REPORT
FROM THE

CONFLUENCE

REPORT FROM THE CONFLUENCE

new poems by

STACIE SMITH

SHANTI ARTS PUBLISHING

BRUNSWICK MAINE

REPORT FROM THE CONFLUENCE
New Poems

Published by Shanti Arts Publishing

Cover and interior design
by Shanti Arts Designs

Cover image by Stacie Smith

Shanti Arts LLC
Brunswick, Maine
www.shantiarts.com

Printed in the United States of America

ISBN: 978-1-951651-67-1

LCCN: 2021931780

In memory of my parents,
Audrey Lucille Fehler Smith
&
Amedee Mellier Smith III

"The farthest star and the mud at our feet are a family; and there is no decency or sense in honoring one thing, or a few things, and then closing the list. The pine tree, the leopard, the Platte River, and ourselves—we are at risk together, or we are on our way to a sustainable world together. We are each other's destiny."

— Mary Oliver, from the essay "Winter Hours" in her book *Upstream*

Also by Stacie Smith

Open Burning

Meanwhile the Earth:
Poems from Cougar Creek

Real News

Second Sight
(a collaboration with June Campbell Rose)

CONTENTS

Where the Pearl Resides

BUILDING A FIRE 17

REPORT FROM THE CONFLUENCE 18

WHERE THE PEARL RESIDES 20

QUARANTINE 22

STILL THERE 24

THAT FRAGRANCE 25

NEW ROOM 26

FALLING ANYWAY 27

GRAIN OF SALT 28

WHAT THE EARTH DOES BEST 29

DARKEST DAY 31

AGREEMENT 32

YELLOW SPIDER 33

JULY 2020 34

RAIN IN AUGUST 35

Symbiosis

YACHATS 39

BASALT 40

WHAT WOULD HAPPEN 41

WILLAMETTE RIVER, WINTER 2018 42

EXHORTATION TO A
    DESPONDENT SELF 43

IDEA 44

HOW NOT TO LIE 45

SYMBIOSIS 46

DRY 47

OUR TREK 48

CURRENCY 50

THE KITE 51

CHRISTMAS EVE 2019 52

NEW YEAR'S EVE 2019 53

A DREAM 54

The Possibility

RENDEZVOUS 59

THE VARIED THRUSH 60

TRY TO TELL 61

EVEN THE HUNGER 62

MIGRATION 63

WHAT THIS MOMENT 64

THE FIELD NEXT DOOR 65

TWO STORMS 66

RIDGELINE TRAIL II 68

VAUX'S SWIFTS: FALL MIGRATION 69

ELK TRAIL 70

THE POSSIBILITY 72

COHO 73

COULD IT BE 74

YACHATS RIVER TRAIL 76

Flesh on the Bones

OUTRAGEOUS DAY 81
TRY ANYWAY 82
LOVE SONG FOR TERRA 83
HAWTHORN 84
LOOK AT ME 86
FOR HER 88
EVENTUALLY THE WORLD 89
ELEGY FOR KASI 90
RISOTTO 91
REASON'S RHYME 92
ROCK CREEK 94
LITTLE ANSWERS 95
STILL AMONG US 96
FLESH ON THE BONES 98
SWEET BURDEN 99

ABOUT THE AUTHOR 101

I.

Where the
Pearl Resides

BUILDING A FIRE

Start with yesterday's news.
Over that, lay kindling
cross-hatched like a small pyre.
Strike a match.

If the kindling is good and dry,
flame will spread from paper
to wood, and that reunion
will warm the air around it.

Suppose the headlines say
the end is near; doesn't matter
to a fire's propensity to burn
whatever's in its path.

Left untended a flame will die.
Too much wood can smother it.
If the fire fades, blow at its base
where coals pulse red and gold.

Be like a bellows or the wind.
Help the blaze grow.

REPORT FROM THE
CONFLUENCE

—Cougar Creek Series LV

Now the human world
is upside down, but
my beloved Elsewhere
still stands right side up,
carrying on with spring.

Bracken ferns unfurl,
no one is there to see.
Bleeding Hearts beat,
no one is there to hear.
Tall wild grasses sway
in a green-scented wind.
Oxalis, Thimbleberry
and Solomon's Seal
all in bright new leaf.
Cougar Creek flows
down and down
toward its confluence
with Elkhorn Creek
which further on
joins Beaver Creek

which then meanders
through the wetlands
to the sea.

The so-called news
is not so good these days.
Touch and travel are proscribed
so my attention turns instead
toward the confluence.
There, my mind's eye sees
what's really happening.

WHERE THE PEARL RESIDES

If what the pundits say is true
we're doomed
unless we move
to higher ground
but I say
higher ground's
already underfoot —
we just don't see —
so we run and run
and run toward
some other place
we think we need to be
when all along
the ease we seek
is in the very
air we breathe.

If what the pundits say is true
we're doomed —
but maybe fear
is where the pearl resides
and all that's left
for us to do
is look inside

and find what's
hidden there —
it might reveal
another way
of being here
and if our days
are numbered
as they say
why not spend them
giving everything
we think we need
away?

QUARANTINE

Which urge to defer to? The one nudging me
onto the road, or the one pointing the way
to the river? Two kinds of movement —
both forbidden now — feet on the ground
left, right, left — or the other, floating,
carried along, the only effort required of me
is to notice this buoyancy and not resist.

Today, something resembling the Plague
besets us, and the road is strewn with
bodies of soldiers who died in the name
of this nation or that, still clutching
their weapons, still holding banners
and flags that signify folly.

I know from my time in the hole
reprieve does come eventually —
a change of guards, a shaft of light
through the window bars, a message
of hope written in a foreign hand,
a flash of sweet oblivion, respite from fear.

Some things come easier now that I'm old—
laughter in the face of hard facts,
impersonal love for the day as it is,
forgiveness—for we know not what we do.
From inside this cell, my mind's-eye,
hurricane-eye, I see the pink hyacinth bloom.

STILL THERE

—Lockdown Series I

The museum is closed
but the treasures within
are still there, radiant,
sheltered in place,
spreading their contagion
of beauty.

These days the air
is thick with dread
but from the balconies
of cities in lockdown,
arias, anthems,
joyful defiant song.

The canals of Venice
are now bluer,
home once again
to dolphins.

THAT FRAGRANCE

—Lockdown Series II

They say today could be our dying day
but I got up this morning anyway
and brewed a cup of China tea
then lit a candle for our world of hurt.

Who am I to question why reality
unfolds the way it does?
If there's anybody left to dig my grave
I want my epitaph to say "She tried."

Outside my door the cottonwoods
exude their bittersweet perfume.
I've loved that fragrance all my life.
I won't stop now.

NEW ROOM

—Lockdown Series III

I enter the stillness of a new room.
Heavy doors close behind me.
Motes of bright dust, like pollen,
swirl in shafts of light that shine
through high windows.

The walls of my cell are stone,
but luminous, like alabaster
lit from within. I've been
sentenced to die here alone,
with no one to share my laughter.

Outside in the free world it's said
there's not enough of anything,
anywhere—the only abundance
is human fear. Meanwhile
spring burgeons, flowers bloom.

FALLING ANYWAY

—Lockdown Series IV

I've been doing my best
trying to keep my distance
as required by the times,
but I'm falling anyway—
onto that slippery slope
toward union.

It could be fatal, falling in love
in this time of contagion,
but prudence be damned—
this world of hurt wants me,
my presence, my touch,
my unmasking.

GRAIN OF SALT

—Lockdown Series V

Mid-April now, time for me
to learn a higher knowing.
My own is insufficient
to these lethal times.

Science tries its best to tell us why
this scourge behaves the way it does.
I respect the explanations but
I take them with a grain of salt.

Tulips the color of blood,
their petals open wide,
give evidence that beauty
coexists with pain.

The earth does what it must.

WHAT THE EARTH DOES BEST

—*Lockdown Series VI*

Days before the pestilence began
I planted seeds—some of my favorites—
cosmos, zinnias, love-in-the-mist.
Then suddenly and everywhere,
death and fear of death abounding.

Where I live, here beside a creek
on the edge of town, if it weren't for
the daily news, I wouldn't know
what's going on beyond my door,
beyond this little patch of ground,
because what I pay attention to
—primarily—is spring unfolding.

Rhododendrons bloom profusely.
Birds are busy building their nests.
Squirrels take from my garden
whatever they can use—all activities
in sync with what the earth does best.

Those seeds I planted need a spell
in lightless time if they're to grow.
It's hard to wait in faith while

germination happens underground
and out of sight. But if I believe in
only what I see, then I'll be blind
to other possibilities. I want to learn
to trust the dark to do its holy deed.

DARKEST DAY

—Lockdown Series VII

Rain and rain and yet more rain —
all night long and still this morning
and into the long dark day.
The creek outside my door
is full to overflowing.

I've been told to stay inside
no matter rain or shine, and
like my neighbors, I comply.
But we're hungry now for touch
and the pleasure of proximity
to friends and even strangers.
Behind our brave masks,
this new kind of sadness.

Rumi says "Our tears improve the earth."
Somewhere, a reservoir is happy.

AGREEMENT

—Lockdown Series VIII

In agreement with this harsh unfolding,
I offer up whatever's left of me, here,
on the ground that spawned me.
I don't know what else to do.
Whatever this moment wants of me,
here I am, at the mercy of mystery.

YELLOW SPIDER

—Lockdown Series IX

A yellow spider rides a spear-shaped leaf.
She's motionless beside a bead of dew.
If I'm quiet long enough, I wonder—
might I see her take a drink?
A little gust of wind creates a stir,
the spider rides the swaying frond,
time stands still.

Meanwhile the human world spins out
its sorry storyline—drama, endless war,
and suffering. But the yellow spider—
for the moment—takes my mind away
from all of that, and for an instant,
beautiful minutia has me in its spell,
reminding me: there's nothing truer
than these tiny silent happenings
no human words can tell.

JULY 2020

—Lockdown Series X

Born not knowing who I am
I gradually become myself
as circumstance determines
how and what I see, and how
and what I understand.

Travel is proscribed these days
and so is touch, but notice how
my feet touch ground, and how
my hands touch one another—
the classic gesture of prayer.

A dark shadow passes overhead
then the gleaming beak of a crow—
one more shard of unbidden beauty—
doing its best to inform me.

RAIN IN AUGUST

Just enough to rinse off summer's dust,
today's surprising rain sweetens the ground,
releasing a musky fragrance — familiar,
potent, necessary — pure antidote
to this drought that besets us,
this estrangement from source.

Meanwhile there's nowhere left for us to go
but in and down, down through the strata —
fear, sorrow, anger, thirst — to where
the great good bedrock heart
is always beating.

II.

Symbiosis

YACHATS

—Series IV

A sunbow appears then fades
out beyond the pewter-grey horizon line.
Nearer shore, monstrous waves
topped by wind-drift fly far and high
like manes of wild horses tossing
in an even wilder sky.

On dark sand, smooth wet stones
the size of small moons the color
of thunder and dusk lie silent
as if stunned by having been hurled
so improbably far by forces so potent
only nature can explain.

BASALT

Stones
have their stories.
Listen: this one
—basalt—
born of fire
then smoothed
in the river
by aeons of time
tumbling
downstream,
landing here
dark and cool
in my hand,
warming slowly
to my touch,
exuding quiet
unknowable knowing,
its provenance
the stars.

WHAT WOULD HAPPEN

—Cougar Creek Series XLIX

Frost has stayed on the meadow
all day long; the new year begins
with winter-browned grasses wearing
cloaks of ice, each spear upright,
sheathed in crystal, and glistening.

What would happen if ambition learned
to shift its gaze away from self, toward
the way the day at hand unfolds?
Could it learn to emulate the way
the grasses shed their cloaks of ice,

the way the grasses, softened by the freeze
and having made their pollen and their seed,
at last lie down, and so become a blanket
for their progeny? What would happen
if we emulated nature's generosity?

WILLAMETTE RIVER,
WINTER 2018

Tufts of plant debris cling to branches
far above the water-line, showing us
how high the river rose last night—
pale flags, ghosts of their former selves,
ripped from places where they had grown
supple and green and firmly attached
to the ground where they first took root,

and now as the flood subsides,
here they are, far above ground,
uprooted and hung out to dry,
all pointing one way—
the way the river reshaped them,
all saying the same thing:
learn from us.

EXHORTATION TO A DESPONDENT SELF

Follow your feelings down and down.
Stay with them, I beg you; see how they beckon,
the way a glance from a beautiful stranger can,
her eyes sparking yours from across the room,
igniting your body with something familiar,
unbidden, and true. Agree to this yearning.
What is it? What does it want you to know?
Something ineffable seeking its name?
Something long-hidden, ready to be found?
Nothing to lose, nothing to gain. Your heart
has a mind of its own; raise your white flag.
The day as it is, replete with your pain
and unknowing, invites your surrender.

IDEA

A bright idea though voiceless at first
eventually finds a mind to reside in
just as a seed carried aloft by wind
sooner or later finds a place to land.

It seems there are madmen at the helm
but meanwhile in a parallel realm
and equally real, a seed has landed
on welcoming ground, sending its roots
down and down into darkness.

HOW NOT TO LIE

Sun shines through my open door
casting shadows on the empty page,
shadows on the day at hand.
Bamboo windchimes clatter
in the early August breeze.

All day I've waited for a word or two
to come along to say the thoughts
that occupy my speechless mind,
but now that I've begun to learn
how not to lie, nothing rings true
but silence.

SYMBIOSIS

Trees inhale my exhalations,
using what my blood unloads
into the bellows of my lungs;
a symbiosis I can't live without.

These poems are just thoughts
conveyed by words that ride my breath;
these words become the exhalations
of my meaning-seeking mind.

Speech requires my breathing out—
another symbiosis I can't live without,
not happily at least; this human being
has a mind that needs to see, then say.

Thought alone is nothing, just as green
and growing things without the necessary
stuff to photosynthesize can't breathe.
Thought needs words and words need me.

DRY

I know the well is dry
but I come to it anyway,
day after day
letting the bucket down.

My neighbors watch.
They shake their heads.
"Poor woman can't accept
the hard reality of drought."

I know this thirst is real.
I've given up explaining.
The memory of water
helps me stay alive.

OUR TREK

Nothing seemed right
when we looked around
at the place where we'd landed —
everything charred, grey, and broken
as far as the eye could see.

We stepped single file
onto the trackless way,
driven by thirst
and unspeakable hunger.

Our trek was hard,
long, and dark.
No one remembered
the towns we had fled.

Someone sang a tune
from the old country.
The music enlivened us.
It sounded like mercy.

We came to a wooden gate.
One of our children opened it.
On the other side, an orchard
of strange flowering trees.

Above these trees, colorful birds
circled high and wide as they sang.
A bright path led to a spring.
The water was clear and abundant.

Some of us wept, all of us vowed
to atone for our sins.
I awoke from that dream,
still weeping.

CURRENCY

Overnight and all at once, the tree outside my door
has dropped its load of gold — I'll stuff my pockets
with this currency, see if it will buy a cup of tea,
a stamp, a book, a loaf of bread.

I have a hunch it won't get far as legal tender.
In an ideal world, it would. But here we are,
swimming in a dream of penury and woe.
Meanwhile, the clouds rain silver.

THE KITE

—Cougar Creek Series L

High in the canopy there's a bird
with a plaintive single-noted call.
Across the way, its mate replies.

Meanwhile on a sandy beach
a child holds the string of a kite.
This is how she learns about wind.

A kite needs wind if it's to fly.
This moment's beauty needs
a beholding eye.

These little thoughts
need a poem to help
say them.

CHRISTMAS EVE 2019

When an undertow hits
and washes the ground
from beneath my feet
I try to remember—
Mary and Joseph
were homeless too.
The exceptional darkness
of that night became home
to the brightest star.

When the discomfort
of emptiness hits me
I try to remember—
Mary agreed to the task.
Being swept out to sea
might be mercy at work.
This bereftness might be
a Bethlehem waiting
for Jesus to come.

NEW YEAR'S EVE 2019

—Cougar Creek Series LIII

Clear-cuts scar the Coast Range
as far as the eye can see.
There's no stopping us.

Lately friends come to me
only in my dreams.
I greet them empty-handed.

Salmon-colored clouds appear
in the daybreak sky. Meanwhile
God levels Her gimlet eye
and takes our measure.

A DREAM

If I knew my way home
I'd be there by now.
Instead, I got lost in a dream.

In this dream, a wide bright river
runs high after days of rain.
It flows through a vastness,
unpeopled and wild.

I've heard it said that
everything in a dream
is the dreamer herself.
I don't know.

But I do know this —
I awoke feeling nourished
and deeply refreshed,
realigned in ways
I didn't even know I craved.

Or maybe the dream
swallowed and digested me
and fed me to the starry night
then spat me out here —

what's left of me — dazed
and oddly fortified,
into the waking day.

Whatever happened, though —
that river and the numinous place
it flowed through — they are real.
I just don't know how to
tell about them.

III.

The Possibility

RENDEZVOUS

—Cougar Creek Series XLIV

Musing on the so-called news
while hiking up the creek-side trail
I was startled back into the moment
by a tiny iridescent hummingbird
who hovered for an instant
inches from my face, her beak
a needle and her wings a blur,
her eyes like tiny onyx beads
mistaking me for something good —
a huckleberry blossom or perhaps
some other nectar-bearing bloom —
and then as suddenly as she'd appeared
she zoomed away so fast and far and high
I felt as if our rendezvous had been a dream
but when we looked each other in the eye
her penetrating glance was fierce and real
and wild and free and made me wonder —
and I wonder still —
what is it nature wants of me?

THE VARIED THRUSH

I never learned to play the violin but
I do know how to fiddle my time away
here in the realm of false refuge
where distractions abound.

A poet I love said something like this:
we humans love coverings; we think
those designs on our curtains
are what the curtains conceal!

As I sat thinking about this,
a Varied Thrush flew hard and fast
against my window—an invisible wall
abruptly ending its life of flight.

If a wall it cannot see
can break a Thrush's neck
because the bird is unaware
that such a thing as glass exists

what fate awaits us wingless ones,
dazzled as we are by what we make
and blind to walls we cannot see,
distracted by the coverings, away
from what lies hidden underneath?

TRY TO TELL

—Cougar Creek Series XLVII

A glossy beetle
black and slick with rain
lumbers slow and sure
across the sodden trail.
Silent golden trumpets rise
from underneath a cloak
of moss and fallen leaves.

Lucky me to be here
noting wonders such as these.
I wish everyone
could see this beetle
and these chanterelles.
I guess it's up to me
to try to tell.

EVEN THE HUNGER

No one is home
to answer my call
so I ask the morning air—
what's to be done
when trail's gone cold?

Ever the sleuth,
my clue-seeking mind
finds nothing these days
but ancient scat,
footprints erased
by wind and silence,
a blade of grass bent
by the tread of a beast
whose name I've forgotten.
Even the hunger
that prompted the hunt
is quiet now.

I wait for a whisper,
a beckon, a sign.
But there's nothing—
only this slow dawning,
this strange new terrain,
this absence of want.

MIGRATION

Long before seeing them, I hear their cries.
I look up and up. There they are—

in fluid formation
and up so high
countless hundreds
could be thousands
of Canada Geese
in undulating
calligraphic lines
a kind of scripture
flowing north
telling a story
about how it is
to be pulled
by a yearning
so mighty
it can't be denied

WHAT THIS MOMENT

A tired old poet with nothing left to say
wandered into the woods at night.
From high in the canopy, two owls
called back and forth, back and forth,
piercing the dark with wild meaning.
The poet moved deeper into a place
where words grow wings ephemeral
as human thought, then fly away.
Meanwhile the owls' query filled the air:
"Who? Who?"

The poet found a place to stop and rest
and ponder what the raptors' song
might possibly be trying to convey.
As darkness dovetailed into light,
the poet heard a wren, a thrush,
a chickadee, a crow.
She dipped her brush into the stream
and then she wrote:
"This moment tells me
everything I need to know."

THE FIELD NEXT DOOR

A new species of thought
caught my eye, then
flew off out of sight,
leaving questions
I don't know how to ask.

Where I lived as a child,
meadowlarks sang
in the field next door.
That field is gone,
that memory, ineffable.

Prayer flags flutter.
Windchimes ring
in response to the breeze.
Meanwhile the crow prevails,
the vulture, the absence of song.

TWO STORMS

One true thing was the sound
of last night's heavy rain,
and the creek as it surged
and roiled in response.

What wasn't so true
was the noise in my head —
another kind of deluge —
backwash chatter-storm
flash-flood of my brain
in hyper-drive: afterimages
from previous waking days
and imaginings of days to come.

I lay there in darkness,
window open to the loud
watery night, suspended
between two storms —
one turning the waterwheel
of my mind, and the other,
more credible — a downpour
accompanied by hard wind.

I fell back asleep to the sound
of my breath, another true thing,
glad for the freedom to choose
which storm to believe.

RIDGELINE TRAIL II

Queen Anne rules this August day.
Her lace is scattered everywhere
and carelessly across the dry terrain.
Cicadas screech and black flies buzz.
A Stellar's Jay proclaims itself the boss
of all that it surveys but meanwhile, circling
high above, a red-tailed hawk says otherwise,
and in my small and wingless mind a kind of
sun-drenched lassitude and curiosity prevails —
if I became that creature's prey, I wonder —
would I have the will to even try to get away?
How would it feel to suddenly be gripped by
talons sharp and strong enough to lift me up
and carry me away from everything I thought I knew,
and in that final conscious instant, fly?

VAUX'S SWIFTS: FALL MIGRATION

—Agate Hall Chimney, Eugene, Oregon, 9/13/2019

Hundreds of us wingless ones
have gathered here to witness
this phenomenon as fading daylight
dovetails into dusk; Vaux's Swifts
in swirling clouds that first condense,
then dissipate, and then condense again
circling clockwise, then in random,
pulsing whorls, some kind of mystifying
choreography, beyond our human ken.

Against the darkening sky the Swifts begin
to form a sort of funnel cloud as if in answer
to a curfew call; it's time to come inside
and rest until the morning's light.
And then the massive ancient chimney
that once billowed smoke now seems
to run the movie in reverse, as countless
valiant little migratory birds are swallowed
into safety for the night.

ELK TRAIL

—Cougar Creek Series LI

Where a herd of elk came down through
the meadow toward Elkhorn Creek
they cut a muddy swath in ground
already tenderized by alternating rounds
of rain and frost.

I followed their trail as far as I could,
to the bank of the winter-swollen creek
where their story line was broken
like a spell—where did they go?

The water itself offered no clue—
clear and unperturbed, all hoof prints
washed away toward Ona Beach
where the creek flows out to sea.

Across Elkhorn I saw where the trail
picked up again on the other side—
a steep, dark, and ragged track
aiming up and up toward the higher wild.

Should I follow? If I do, and don't return,
who would know what had lured me off
and far away? Could anyone imagine
where I might have gone?

All life long I've sought my tribe.
I haven't found it yet—the elks' trajectory
that leads me to the spawning stream
might be as close as I will ever get.

THE POSSIBILITY

All indicators point to our demise
so I walk the Ridgeline Trail each day
because it's always steady under foot.
Early winter now; rosehips shrivel
on the leafless bush, while hawks
and jays and hardy little chickadees
accompany my flights of mind
as I seek remedy for human folly —
mostly mine.

Discomfort — strangely — comforts me.
Familiar, so reliable, so always there,
a kind of temple bell that serves to say
longevity might not be everything
that it's cracked up to be!
Breathe out, breathe in, hold steady
as she goes, step lightly on the path
and contemplate the possibility
that no one really knows!

COHO

—Cougar Creek Series LIV

Moss hangs wet and heavy
from the branches
of a broadleaf maple tree.
Droplets form. Within them
tiny inverse worlds appear
before they fall.

Through one such lens
just look — beneath a bridge
that spans the creek — a Coho
pale and spent from spawning
now decaying in the very place
where it was born.

Wedged against the bank,
the tattered carcass undulates
as water passes overhead.
That noble corpse tells everything
there is to know about the mystery
that can't be said.

COULD IT BE

cat on the sill
spider in its web
shadow on the page

done with false refuge
and priming the pump
done with running

beyond my door
the big picture
reels out unchecked

the cosmos condensed
in the moment at hand
nothing to be done

people say otherwise
this cause or that
needs you

but i say pay heed
to everything equally
nowhere left to go

one breath at a time
could it be peace
has no contingencies?

YACHATS RIVER TRAIL

Long vertical wounds ooze fresh sap
where a Cougar sharpened its claws
—quite recently—on the slender trunk
of a young fir, digging all the way
through its bark into the white
fibrous flesh underneath.
If I come back tomorrow
I'll see the sap has hardened
to become a crystal scab.

I walk this trail most days without
concern but now this evidence
—raw slashes still dripping tree-blood—
stops me in my tracks and now
I sense a lethal possibility—
the Cat who left these stripes
knows this trail better than I do
and it has newly sharpened claws
and it is hungry.

IV.

Flesh on
the Bones

OUTRAGEOUS DAY

Today I walk the creek-side trail
and notice that there's no one else around.
I don't mind solitude but truth be told
I'd rather not be solo when I hear
the sweetgums screaming bloody crimson,
see cottonwoods and maples blazing gold.
This day is violent with splendor —
I can't bear it on my own. Sometimes
I need protection from my senses —
they assault me with the beauty they behold.

At times like this I think of Vincent,
and I wonder — was he mad, or just a victim
of extraordinary sight? Did he hear the stars?
Did he suffer from inordinate delight?
With no way to quench his appetite
for heaven here on earth — that field of wheat,
that wooden chair, the reeling sky, the night café —
he turned to color; only color could begin to tell
about the numinous extravagance of tulips,
those undulating cypress trees, the unspeakably
outrageous day.

—*for Vincent van Gogh*

TRY ANYWAY

It can't be said,
but the wind and tides
try anyway.
So do the limpet
and whale.
What I want to say
can't be said
without consulting
the recently dead.

I hear them say:
This toxic plague
runs far and fast
and wide and deep.
Your desire to stop it
might seem a lost cause,
a candle in the wind.
Try anyway.

—*for Rachel Carson*

LOVE SONG FOR TERRA

—Cougar Creek Series LVI

This longing for words
to tell about you
leaves me speechless

but your dark eyes
loosen my tongue.

Because of your kindness
I want to be kind.

Because you forbear my folly
I'll be your fool.

Because you forgive
I'll repent.

HAWTHORN

Severance pay was not enough
to save her from the streets
but why even mention it
when the air is already
so thick with need?
If I turn my pockets
inside out to show
I too am severed
from the mainstream
does that feeble gesture
feed a single soul?
This question pulls me
up the hill to Hawthorn,
remedy for ailments
of the human heart.
White blossoms drift down
from branches soon to be
laden with berries
the color of blood.
I know of no solution
to our existential woes
but Hawthorn does:
Defer to the seasons.
Put down roots.

Offer up the fruits
of your being.

—for the homeless woman in the parking lot

LOOK AT ME

My name is Ana Maria
Claudia
Elaine
Maryanne

Look at me

My name is Lillie
Sally
Deborah
Ann

Don't look away

My name is Cherie
Carolyn
Judith
Charlotte

Look me in the eye

My name is Teresa
Erin
Jacqueline
Jan

My name is
your mother
your sister
your daughter

Look at me
Don't look away

     —for Dr. Christine Blasey Ford

FOR HER

Now that my senses have come home to me
my body tells me what I need to know—
this flash of fear says Danger,
and like a startled fawn, I spring to safety
without pausing to ask why.

This knowing speaks a tongue once forbidden
but now I say and say and say:
no one—not even the giant at the gate—
can stop me. Victim long enough
and done with that.

    —for J.A., survivor

EVENTUALLY THE WORLD

In her later years, she said,
she left her door unlocked
to see who she could meet.
She was done with deadbolts,
locks and keys—without them
she felt happier, she said, and free.
Eventually the world
would find her anyway.

Unspeakable intrusions
taught her as a child
to move toward the hidden,
toward the beautiful and right.

She said she learned to merge
with what she loved to see—
the fawn, the spider in its web,
the fox and snail and wren
and other quiet denizens of earth.
When asked to name a favorite word
she laughed and said there are so many!
Constancy, for instance, praise,
and love, and mirth.

    —after reading an interview with Mary Oliver

ELEGY FOR KASI

Pure intention drove her digging.
I never saw her catch her prey
but she tried and tried and tried,
returning home with shining eyes,
mud-encrusted nose and paws,
and smiling.

As her muzzle whitened over time
her puppy-nature grew unchecked.
A mix of Vizsla hound and rascal
she was willful, loyal, kind, and swift.
I mourn her passing more than
words can say.

My mind's-eye sees her wag
and dash and leap, and now
she nourishes the ground
where grasses will grow taller
than before. May she dig
and run forever in sacred sleep.

RISOTTO

No one knows this ragged little town
or loves it better than my brother does.
He knows its secrets and its shames.
His response to all of it is generosity.
You'll find him in the kitchen
making something nourishing and good.

He takes the folly of the world to heart
but stays attentive to the task at hand —
there's risotto to be stirred, and stirred,
    and stirred . . .
He's a poet's poet, master chef and hermit monk,
possessed of an encyclopedic mind, a man
who shows us what it looks like to be kind.

—for Amedee

REASON'S RHYME

Words about water
can't douse a flame
so why write verse
when the world's on fire?

Paradise is lost.
What good is song?
At times like this
what good is any art?

Not rhetorical,
these questions
that unsettle any
thinking heart.

No one knows
exactly why
a day unfolds
the way it does

but neither time
nor holocaust can kill
the heart's desire
for reason's rhyme.

   —*for the victims of the Camp Fire, northern
   California, 2018*

ROCK CREEK

No human word can say exactly
how it feels to flow downhill
as Rock Creek does when it obeys
the laws of gravity that guide it down
and over and around all obstacles
toward the sea — but any devotee
of mystery will find some way
to praise.

To try to tell about the way it feels
to love how water moves toward the sea
is to be lifted up into that mystery
where music rides the wind
and fills the stream and flows
into and through the Diva,
and she cannot help but sing,
and singing, lift us up
and carry us along.

      —in memory of Aretha Franklin

LITTLE ANSWERS

After reading Chuang-tzu
little questions come to me—
Who was his mother?
Did he ever have a wife?
A favorite auntie, or a sister
or a girl next door?
Who were the nurturers
of his vast mind?

I put the book aside
and turn toward
the day at hand.
Little answers drift my way—
Shadow on the page.
Windchime ringing.
Black fly buzzing,
Sword ferns glistening.

—after reading a translation by Burton Watson

STILL AMONG US

A rumor — at first distant and vague —
like thunder high and far away
then nearer and louder
then overhead and all around

a white man's knee
on a Black man's neck

his cries for his mama
his desperation to breathe

mama mama

then outrage igniting
furious righteous grief
and rage multiplied
and erupting
it won't be stopped
not this time

any mother
anywhere
who saw him
being killed
who heard his

dying words
will vow
with her life
to protect
those children
still among us

 —in honor of George Floyd

FLESH ON THE BONES

My world is small but it teems with angels.
It could fit on the head of a pin—my sons
and their children, my siblings and theirs,
my neighbors and friends—altogether,
how much do their souls weigh?
As much as that pale blue feather that fell
from above and drifted into my open hand
the morning we were rescued from the flood?

Where I live, such miracles play out every day.
My job is to try to tell about the ones I see.
So I turn to this thin page, the moment at hand.
Whatever brought me here into this world of hurt
wants me to do my best to say whatever small thing
my heart knows to be true. Words fail me but
they're all I have—courage, blood, justice,
peace—to help put flesh on the bones of love.

        —in honor of John Lewis

SWEET BURDEN

Backlit by afternoon sunlight
the bodies of honeybees glow
like amber beads with wings,
their leg sacs stuffed with gold,
their purposeful movements
causing blossoms to tremble.

Every single minute, those bees
know what to do; gather pollen,
harvest nectar, return to the hive,
unpack their sweet burden, then
fly out and do that again and again
and again, as long as daylight lasts.

This little tale sounds too simple,
too pure for these deadly times, but
I'll say it anyway, if for no one's ears
but mine; I need to see and tell about
the way some creatures keep on doing
what is good, delicious, and right.

   —for all essential workers

ABOUT THE AUTHOR

Stacie Smith is a fourth generation Oregonian. This is her fifth book of poems. She lives in her home town, Eugene, Oregon, in the Willamette River valley.

SHANTI ARTS

NATURE ▪ ART ▪ SPIRIT

Please visit us online
to browse our entire book catalog,
including poetry collections and fiction,
books on travel, nature, healing, art,
photography, and more.

Also take a look at our highly
regarded art and literary journal,
Still Point Arts Quarterly, which may
be downloaded for free.

www.shantiarts.com

CPSIA information can be obtained
at www.ICGtesting.com
Printed in the USA
FSHW021732170821
83879FS